How to Le
Squarespace Quickly

Andrei Besedin

Table of Contents

Table of Contents _____ 2

Introduction _____ 7

    Understanding Squarespace _____9

Chapter 1 _____ 11

Starting Your Website _____ 11

    1.   Selecting a Template _____11

    2.   Account Creation_____11

    3.   Get Accustomed with the Websites Backend _____12

    4.   Structuring the Basic Info _____13

    5.   Navigation and Page Setups _____15

    6.   Site Customization _____15

    7.   Going Live _____16

Chapter 2 _____ 18

5 Things to Observe When You Begin Your Squarespace 14 Days Trial_____ 18

    The Templates _____19

    Mobile Response _____21

    Scope _____22

    Backends _____23

App Connection _____23

Chapter 3 _____ 25

How to Style Your Website _____ 25

What the Style Editor Does _____25

Typographical Aspect_____27

Chapter 4 _____ 33

A Detailed Guide on How to Set up Blocks Pages and
Navigation in Squarespace _____ 33

Navigation _____33

Considerations to make when Starting Your Navigation __35

Pages_____36

Considerations to Make When Starting your Page_____38

Page Customization _____40

Essentials _____41

Picture Designs_____43

Displays _____44

Synopsis _____45

More_____46

Channels and Records _____48

Trade_____49

Outlines _____50

Social _____50

Considerations to Make When Starting your Block _____51

Chapter 5 _____ *54*

5 Quick Customization Methods for Your Squarespace Site
_____ *54*

    Block Resizing_____55

    Customizing your Headers_____56

    Navigation Dropdown Customization_____56

    Customize your Buttons, Graphics, and Borders _____56

    Add a Favicon _____57

Chapter 6 _____ *59*

*7 Actions to Take Once your Squarespace Website Goes
Live* _____ *59*

    Essential Information and Business _____59

    SEO (Search Engine Optimization)_____60

    Photos_____61

    Social Media Networks _____62

    404 Error Pages _____63

    Post Your New Website on Your Social Media Networks _64

    Consider Your Website as Unfinished_____64

*Conclusion*_____ *66*

By reading this document, the reader agrees that under no circumstances is the author responsible for any losses, direct or indirect, that are incurred as a result of the use of information contained within this document, including, but not limited to, errors, omissions, or inaccuracies.

Introduction

If you're looking for the ideal platform to create an excellent website effortlessly, Squarespace is a perfect option. It comes with a simple interface that allows individuals with small scale businesses to have an online platform to showcase their businesses.

Many people running into millions have utilized this incredible platform to create a website of their preference. The number of users keeps rising as the days pass.

The simplicity and the various options of the Squarespace platform are so extraordinary that users don't need to be experts on building websites to make use of this platform.

Due to the easy built-in tools available, anyone without coding expertise can build a quality website. The content running and the web hosting of this platform comes together in one subscription to work efficiently.

The systems of most platforms differ as they prefer the content running and web hosting to be on different subscriptions. Some other platforms even implement subsequent security updates to be carried out by the user.

Squarespace makes sure that all the securities on every site on their platform is well updated and in order, making it possible for the users on the platform to face the running of their websites with ease. All the websites all utilize the same content running as provided by the Squarespace platform.

All the websites on the platform all utilize the same functions irrespective of the different subscriptions. Some of the subscriptions will enable some sites to have a restricted number of pages, while others will have innovative e-commerce features.

As time goes on, regular updates are introduced by Squarespace and the incorporation of new advanced features. You can check their website to find out the available prices for all their plans and subscriptions.

As we advance in this book, we will discuss their templates and features. Due to the regular updates made available by Squarespace, their information contents are always well updated with the latest updates, features, and templates.

It is why this book focuses on teaching you all the essentials you need to know to help you utilize the Squarespace platform more efficiently and effectively.

The knowledge you will acquire from this book will also help you know everything about the Squarespace platform, including their current updates, features, templates, and future ones.

Understanding Squarespace

Squarespace is a platform used for website creation. They gained their popularity from the all-in-one characteristics they used in building their simple system. Another area they also excel highly is in the designing of top-grade templates and sophisticated features for all the various websites.

WordPress and Squarespace, which is better?

There is no specific characteristic that makes one better than the other; however, it depends on the preference of the user and whichever type of organization they want.

Most users that run small scale businesses and most experts prefer Squarespace. It is mostly because most of these small-scale businesses don't work with a consistent IT division. It is the work of the IT division to help with website creation and maintenance; however, most of these small businesses do not have a lot of staff, and that's probably the reason for the lack of an IT division.

Squarespace is a complete all-in-one platform that has a team of experts that are in charge of the security updates and upgrading of the back-end systems to help with the SEO drills and systems update.

The user doesn't need to do much work; the entire user needs to get used to is learning how to use the

Squarespace blocks and move them around. With this knowledge, a user can easily create a page and post information on it.

It doesn't mean that other website platforms like the likes of WordPress and Shopify are not quality websites. They, however, focus on a different category of customers. I

t is why I suggest that WordPress and Shopify are best for large scale businesses that require a vast majority of website functions like online shops that make use of the user's login details, forums, booking systems with various complexities, and lots more. These complex functions are why many people prefer these systems; however, you shouldn't leave out the fact that these systems all have their issues.

WordPress makes use of various plugins to enable the functionalities. In the case of new updates, they affect the plugins, making them behave erratically. These problems most times can be fixed, but most of the time, it takes a bit of consistent work from a WordPress developer to fix things.

To keep things simple, if you're a creative expert or you're into a small-scale business that doesn't utilize an IT team, Squarespace will be the best option for you.

Chapter 1

Starting Your Website

1. Selecting a Template

Click on Start a Free Trial or the Create a Site button located on the Squarespace Webpage; it will instruct you to select a template. There are over 90 attractive templates on just the Squarespace website. Just remember that these templates are not permanent; they can be changed when necessary.

2. Account Creation

Squarespace gives users a free 14 days trial for their website before they can start subscribing. It's fascinating because other website builders don't do such. During your 14 days trial, you can test out the templates, check out Squarespace's backend to get things actively working before the upgrading and publishing of your website.

You can start the trial by creating an account on Squarespace. Select the template you want to use; then, you'll be asked for some necessary information like your email, first name, last name, password, and address to create your account.

Once you're done with this process, Squarespace will give you a few additional questions like "What is this website about?" "Which title will you use for your website?" and "What goals do you have for this website?" for concluding the basic set-up of your website.

Squarespace will utilize most of these questions in structuring the backend for your website. In contrast, the rest of the items and information will be used by Squarespace to keep records of the users that are making use of their platform.

3. Get Accustomed with the Websites Backend

Once you are done filling in the answers to the questions, Squarespace will immediately direct you into your newly created website. All the tools you require to make any necessary edits on your website are located at the menu on the screens left. You'll also find links that will enable you to manage the various areas of your website.

Pages direct you to your contents

Design gives your website a brilliant and attractive look that it has.

Marketing creates room for tools utilized by social media and emails.

Comments compile the list of comments in one section.

Settings are used to control backend functionalities and contact information.

Help takes you to the knowledge section of Squarespace.

Make sure that you check out these sections for you to gain a better understanding of how your site's backend functionalities work. The live preview of your site is displayed on the right side of this window.

Initially, you'll find a demo of your chosen template in that area, but as you produce more pages, customize contents, and add pictures to your site, the customization of your site upgrades.

Once you scroll on top of the line icon above the window, you will see an arrow appear. Click on the arrow to see a preview of the tablet version, smartphone version, and desktop version of your website. It will help you when creating the design and layout for your website's content.

4. Structuring the Basic Info

Since you are now acquainted with your website's backend, it's ideal for creating the necessary information before commencing with the designs and contents.

The first thing for you to do is to click on **Design**, click **Logo**, and **Title**. The title of your site will become visible, leaving you with the tagline to add. After the tagline, it's time to add an image. The image will take the place of the title of your website, so I'll recommend you make use of your company image or logo.

During the upload, the image should be in an exact quality PNG format with a translucent background. Most of the other templates have scrolling parallax, which means they don't appear to have a white background and it wouldn't be suitable for a white box to appear behind the logo subsequently.

Another essential aspect that is necessary for this area is the favicon, which is a small icon that can be seen in the web bookmarks and the windows of the browser. It is vital to utilize a secondary image suitable for a box shape and readable when arranged small.

Adding a logo for social sharing is also possible; however, it is optional. A display of the social sharing image appears when you want to share your pages with your social media.

Always save your updates by the top side of the screen before going back to the home menu. Once you've gotten to the Home Menu, click **Settings – Basic Information**. Changing the name of the site you entered can also be done on the home menu.

However, the most vital aspect of this part of the screen is the description of the site. Anything your input as the description will be what will pop up when searched for on search engines. It is why you need to make use of the right keywords to help produce better SEO results.

5. Navigation and Page Setups

This part is exciting because this is where the main website building begins. It involves setting up and structuring your web site's navigation and page setup. Since the templates of Squarespace come with a demo layout, it's either you use those layouts in creating your contents, or you erase them and come up with a new one.

There are so many things you'll need to learn about navigation and page setup, extra unlinked page creation, utilizing blocks to create your pages, and many more. I will introduce a guide to you to help you with navigation and page setup as we progress further in this book.

6. Site Customization

Since you're now done with the fundamental structuring of your site, it's time to get on with the designing aspect. First of all, you can go to the **Design** area of the home menu to select the **Style editor**, which makes it possible for you to design your site in a way that will match your content and brand.

The templates in this section vary depending on the organization and styling preferences that are available. It's either you make use of the style editor for font, size, color, and background customizations when it relates to pre-footer, headers, site navigations, primary content, buttons, and footers, or you can alternatively make use of custom code to change your website's design.

7. Going Live

Once you're done with the designing of your website, you'll have to get ready to switch from your 14 days trial by creating a new custom domain, or you move over one that is already existing; for upgrading from your trials, log into your Squarespace website's backend and click on **Settings – Billing and Account – Billing** from the menu that is at the left side of the screen.

The screen will display a large gray button to **Upgrade**; just follow the steps given to you. All your customization will remain intact even after upgrading. Go to **Settings** and click on **Domains** to manage your domain. Squarespace will give your site a default domain at the beginning of your product trial.

After adding a custom domain to your website, a Squarespace.com default domain will display at your backend. You can only see this. It is only the custom domain that will be visible to visitors. The following options will help you set up a custom domain:

- If you use an annual subscription, you can complete the registration of a domain managed by Squarespace by clicking **Get a Domain**.

- If you don't use an annual subscription, you can still buy a domain managed by Squarespace by clicking **Get a Domain**.
- If you already have a domain hosted by another platform, all you must do is link your domain in the **Domain section** by clicking on **Use a domain I own**.

Chapter 2

5 Things to Observe When You Begin Your Squarespace 14 Days Trial

When you plan on deciding, you don't do so in haste; it's essential to make some observations and conduct a test run along the way. No one would love to purchase a vehicle without having to give it a test run spin to ascertain the overall condition of the car.

You wouldn't go for a perfect pair of quality trousers without having to try them on. The same thing goes when it comes to selecting your preferred platform for your website.

Before subscribing to any plan, you should confirm if the platform is ideal and suitable for your business plans; it is why the Squarespace platform is very excellent.

Squarespace gives you a **14 days trial** to test run your website before you make a final decision to commit yourself to a paid plan. During the trial period, you can test your website's features, and even test run the backend.

Interestingly, no credit card is needed to begin your trial. For you to make the best out of your 14 days trial,

I have rounded up some of the five most vital observations to make during your 14 days trial.

The Templates

Squarespace makes a lot of beautiful templates available for your site. All these templates are all customizable, with each of them having their exclusive features.

As you progress on your 14 days trial, it is vital to find out those features that are very necessary for your website. It will make you know what features and templates that will be ideal for you.

These are some of the things you'll need to consider:

Are you a Blog Owner?

If the answer is yes, it's best to add a blog sidebar, so that should be one of the first things for you to consider, is a sidebar going to be suitable for your website?

It's up to you to decide. Which type of metadata will be attached to all your posts? I could be tags, dates, categories, authors, and lots more. It's left for you to decide which is suitable for you.

Most templates don't have a sidebar feature in them; the metadata of every template differs. Most templates are made precisely for blogs, while the other templates are strategically made for e-commerce purposes.

Are You an Online Store Owner?

If the answer is yes, will it be necessary to add a chart on your top navigation or not? Is it vital to add product pictures that produce unique features when you rove around the image? Squarespace makes a lot of these exquisite templates to be specifically suited for online stores; Squarespace will make the products visible in various patterns on all the templates.

Which Style will best Suit your Navigation Menu?

Will you prefer several navigation menus? or will you select a single menu assigned to the top corner on the right or a regular navigation menu spread above? It is what makes the difference between all the templates. Some of these templates have several navigation menus, while the rest do not have many options.

Would photo be a priority?

What do you have in mind for banner images about your site? Is it something that you want? Or do you also plan to add texts to the images? Squarespace has templates that can incorporate beautiful images; however, without a high-quality image to match these templates, it might seem useless.

If you prefer a complete image that is extremely clear, you might want to enlist the help of a professional photographer to help you attain a top quality that will be attractive to visitors. If you're not too concerned with that, then I suggest you go for a template that doesn't feature lots of images

Any Plans for Index Pages?

The index pages are utilized to extract contents and pictures from various pages and add them to a precise location, giving your visitors the ease to keep scrolling down a page.

It doesn't mean all the templates have this feature, which is why I stress the importance of familiarizing with your templates from the beginning to know their specific characteristics.

There are a lot of things to observe, so at times this can be so tedious, especially when you're trying to choose a suitable template. That is why the four questions I listed in this section will help steer you in the right way.

As time goes on, you can customize your website; you can even switch templates whenever you like. But it will be worth it if you have all the necessary features you require on your template. So, make out time to study your template as you try it out during the 14days trial.

Mobile Response

Squarespace has responsive templates, meaning they can work well on smartphones and desktops without you putting in any effort. Though it might not require any action from you, you need to find out if the template for the desktop version is also suitable for the mobile site as well.

For a preview of your site in other versions, hove your mouse over the single line icon above the screen and click the icon for various devices. Some templates will enable you to make changes to the template of your mobile version. Simply visit the style editor to effect those changes.

Scope

Squarespace is the best, most ideal platform for creative and artistic minded individuals. Whenever you are amongst these categories, an artist, a photographer, a musician, a blogger etc.

Squarespace will provide you with everything you need. However, for those of you that have a large-scale business in mind that requires some specific requirements, I wouldn't be surprised if you get disappointed because Squarespace is best suited for small scale businesses.

From your 14 days trial with Squarespace, I believe the platform will meet all your requirements and standards. You should test all the various blocks as you set up your pages.

Test the setup options for the backend and eCommerce. You can start by creating a post to apply all the necessary features required and see if the standards suit your preference before deciding to go for an upgrade.

Backends

Squarespace is known for its user-friendly characteristics. It is so easy for me to recommend it to you because of the simplicity and easy flow. Anything you want to do is done quickly without much fuss.

However, if you're a novice in the area of technology and computers, this might probably take a while for you to adjust.

Take advantage of the trial time to get to know the way the backends of your site works. It's okay to make some new pages, try out the fonts, colors, and other style editor features.

You can also test out various blocks. The site doesn't need to reach a perfection level from the very start; give yourself some room to learn to get the preference you want.

App Connection

Squarespace is different from WordPress because it doesn't utilize plugins for site customization. Though there is great emphasis on the importance of templates, domain, eCommerce, hosting, and others in a single place, it is also vital to make sure your site can connect with various apps.

As you run your 14 days trial, make sure you strategize on getting the precise plugins and apps suitable for your site. You can utilize a site like Zapier as support; however, this is a consideration you'll have to make at the beginning stage of your site construction.

Looking onto the bright side, Squarespace is a closed design for better security. It is why you must utilize the 14 days to go through your website before you decide to subscribe for real.

Have an exciting journey going through your site and carrying out the necessary trials and experiments required. Check out the various templates, try them out on your devices, check out the scope, and ensure they meet your standards.

Try out the backends and ensure everything is for your apps. Once your site is in good shape just the way you like it, then you can go ahead and make an upgrade, which is by the down part of the screen.

Chapter 3

How to Style Your Website

Using the backends and setting up is relatively easy with Squarespace. However, when it comes to the templates' customization, it will require a bit of style and creativity to come up with something that suits perfectly what you want.

Squarespace has made a feature available to enable you to choose various designs and edits, and that feature is known as the Style editor.

What the Style Editor Does

If you're looking to make changes to your sites like changing the font color, spacing, or background, the style editor is the tool that gets the job done.

There are available options in the style editor known as tweaks, and you can make use of these tweaks to see a preview of whatever changes that you want to effect.

The Availability of Tweaks depends on the Template you Decide to Utilize

Most of them don't allow blog sidebars while others do. Some allow the various headers' customization, while some stick to one font for all the header styles.

When choosing your template, it is essential to check

out the style editor to know how many customization options are available before using your website's template. (Start by beginning your free 14 days trial).

Where the Tweaks are Located

The tweaks are dependent on your website pages currently previewed by your screens right side, and they all differ following the type of page.

- Product page
- Cover page
- Event page
- Index page
- Blog page
- Gallery page

Once you make changes for your gallery page utilizing your style editor, it automatically affects your gallery page by altering all the pages. The same thing applies to all the other listed pages.

If you want to edit using the style editor, you must be on the page you plan to edit before opening the style editor. You also need to be aware of the type of page you're editing.

Click on **Design - Style Editor** on the Main Menu.

The tweak options will display on the left part of the screen. However, you can go to the right part of the page to bring out the tweaks meant for those sections.

For instance, if you plan on changing your headers to a different style, all you need to do is click on the text for headers on the preview page.

All the tweaks that are not related to the header will be removed by the style editor for you to make easy changes to the header. To preview all available options, go to the menu on top and click on **Show All.**

Tips: The best option for editing your Squarespace website is either Firefox or Chrome. If you're making use of Safari, the page often reloads from time to time, and this can make you lose all the changes that you plan to effect before you hit the save button.

Some Regular Tweak Styles

Though templates come with various tweaks, their tweaks are also familiar with each other. The templates come with various styles; however, these styles can be changed using the style editor.

Typographical Aspect

The Squarespace font collection comprises Typekit Fonts (1000) and Google Fonts (600). The Menus for the font are arranged in the style editor according to their ranking. To see all the fonts available on the list, scroll down, but if you like to see all the fonts in the font library, you can do so by searching via the menu search space.

The font tweaks are organized into sections like Navigation text, headings, and body text. However, this is adjustable, depending on the type of template you are using.

- Align text (right, left, center)

- Size of Font

- Text Transformation (lowercase, uppercase, none, capitalization)

- Spacing of Letters

- The height of the line (The spacing between every roll of texts)

- The Font

- The Decoration of the Text (Line through, none, underline)

You should know that every change you execute amongst these options above will also reflect on the whole website. For instance, if you decide to change the body text's font size, it will apply to all the entire body texts on your website.

It was a necessary functionality put in place by Squarespace to make sure your site remains in a uniform standard. If you want to customize your fonts, you can make use of Typekit with integrations from Squarespace.

Colors

There are colored circles close to the labels of every colored tweak. To make color changes, click on the colored circle; once you do that, a color picker will be displayed to select a color of your preference from the wheel of colors. Another alternative way of choosing a color is by entering specific values using the following formats:

HTML white, HSL (325, 100%, 59%, 1), RGB (250, 0, 149, 1), HEX (#FFFFFF)

For transparency adjustments, you can utilize the opacity slider. Total transparency is denoted by A, while total Opaque is represented by 1.

Alternatively, you can go underneath the dialogue box and click transparent. If you're done choosing your color, click on any place that is not within the wheel color area to go back to the style editor.

Sizes

Size measurements are in pixel, and they include tweaks like borders, spacing, padding, and width. For size tweak creation, type a number into space or make do with the slider.

Aspect Ratio

This tweak involves the image widths and heights and cropping ratios, for example, a 1x2 Square. In most cases, the aspect ratio is programmed at auto, which means the image will be arranged to suit the page size.

Background Picture

This tweak is not included in all the templates. Most of the templates that include this tweak do have a page background picture.

Click on the circle close to the site's background picture logo to upload your preferred image. You can also include images that are licensed from Getty Images. However, the photos will cost you. Tips for your background picture:

- Squarespace advises the use of a full high-quality background picture of 1500 pixels.

- Images with landscape formats are better than those in portrait format.

- Due to Squarespace's compatibility over various screen sizes and platforms, it can crop background pictures in most cases. So, you should make use of images that do not contain texts.

- Should you decide to change the template of your website; the background picture will not transfer.

Banner Pictures

Just like background pictures, banner pictures are not accessible on all templates. Should a template have a wide site banner, you can use the Style Editor to upload it.

You can include those templates that come with page banners in the page settings. To have a banner picture, click on the circle close to the Background picture header and select a photo from your Getty image Gallery.

SideBar

Not all templates have a sidebar. The templates that have this feature include a sidebar tweak in the style editor, and the options vary depending on the template. To get a sidebar tweak, go to the page preview and click on the sidebar, or you go to style editor and search for the sidebar header.

Hiding and Displaying

You can hide most of your site features like the banners, footers, page descriptions, and social icons. Check under the options area to see the checkmarks of these tweaks.

Saving and Undoing

Any tweak you make using the style editor makes a gray dot visible on the left side of the label. Click on the dot to undo whatever changes you've made. Once you're done with all the changes, scroll to the top, and click on save. The changes will reflect on your site.

If you want to start all over again, you can undo all these changes by going to the bottom of the style editor menu and clicking **Reset** all to default. It will revert your site to the original default of the template.

Chapter 4

A Detailed Guide on How to Set up Blocks Pages and Navigation in Squarespace

Since you've begun your Squarespace preliminary and set up your Squarespace site, it's an ideal opportunity to begin modifying the site to your requirements.

However, before you plunge into the plan, you'll have to construct an establishment for your new site by setting up your Navigation menu, adding pages, and rounding out those pages utilizing blocks.

This post will walk you through the fact that it is easy to manufacture an establishment for your site utilizing Squarespace.

Navigation

The Navigation of your site is a bunch of connections that guide guests to your site content. A Navigation menu ordinarily shows at the highest point of your site, notwithstanding, a few templates uphold Navigation in a sidebar or footbar.

The Primary Navigation

Pages connected in the Primary Navigation are the obvious pages included in the Navigation bar at the highest point of your site.

You'll see that the pattern my pages are recorded in the left-hand segment copies the pattern they're recorded at the highest point of my site.

On the off chance that you'd prefer to switch the patterns for your pages, you can relocate the pages to the pattern you'd lean toward in the left-hand section.

Navigation for the Footer

Pages connected in the Footer Navigation are the obvious pages included in the optional navigation at the lower part of your site (if your template bolsters an auxiliary Navigation).

The pattern for the left-hand board's connections impersonates the pattern they're recorded over the lower part of your site.

If you'd prefer to switch the pattern for your pages, you can virtually move the pages into the pattern you would like.

Not Connected

Not Connected pages will be pages on your site that can't be gotten to from the primary or footer navigation; however, they might be gotten to different aspects of your site.

I would not like to incorporate my Documents page in my Primary Navigation or my Footer Navigation. Yet, I needed to have the option to connect to it in my blog sidebar. I set it up as an unlinked page, and it misses the eyes until the guest taps on its immediate connection in the sidebar of my blog.

Considerations to make when Starting Your Navigation

When discussing the Navigation (or menu as it's regularly approached) on your site, the topic of the number of connections to have in your menu consistently springs up.

I recommend close to six connections. It's more straightforward, less overpowering for your guests, and arranges the data on your site.

You likewise need to make sure to keep the duplicate as necessary and clear as could be expected under the circumstances.

While "About," "Home," "Administrations," "Blog," "Contact," and so forth may appear to be exhausting and abused, your guests will never need to think about what page that connects to.

Navigation Customization

When your Navigation is set up, you can utilize the Style Editor (in the menu for design) to change your Navigation appearance. Each template category has its Style Editor, so the choices accessible for refreshing your Navigation connections can shift.

Look through the changes on the left-hand side and search for changes that incorporate the word Navigation.

A portion of the changes you can make to your navigation incorporates changing the textual style, size, font, shading, position, separating between and around connections, hover choices, and so forth.

For a complete tutorial on styling your navigation, Squarespace has an incredible assistance guideline available.

Pages

Pages are the parts that make up your site and store your resources. You can utilize an assortment of pages to make your site's resources. Contingent upon your template, you have a few page alternatives.

Page

This choice gives you a fresh start where you can add mixes of blocks that structure a custom design of text, pictures, sound, structures, and that's just the beginning. As a result of its adaptability, it's an extraordinary decision for the lion's share of your resources.

Items

This page alternative is tweaked for storekeepers. It permits you to make a page to store the entirety of your items.

Cover Page

A Cover Page permits you to introduce data on a solitary striking page (as a rule with full drain pictures) and make a fantastic prologue to your site. You can even utilize a mix of Cover Pages and Pages to create a unique feel to your site.

Folders

Folders aren't a page, yet they're the key to making a drop-down menu that accommodates a few pages.

Collection

Collection pages permit you to transfer music and enable guests to tune in to your tracks.

File

A File page shows your substance by utilizing thumbnail pictures to connect to pages or arrange display content.

Blog

The Blog page holds an assortment of blog entries.

Functions

The Functions page can be utilized as a schedule or rundown of functions like talking commitment, gatherings, and public functions.

Display

Display pages permit you to exhibit an assortment of pictures and recordings. It is particularly useful for picture takers, originators, and specialists.

Connection

The Connection page isn't a page by the same token. It associates with another site or page inside your site.

Considerations to Make When Starting your Page

When you add a Page to your site, you have two choices: start with a clear record or pick a starter format.

Starter formats are proficient plans for pages with pre-masterminded placeholders. The placeholders give you a thought of what your page may resemble.

By utilizing a starter format, you can fabricate a page using a structured plan for a particular reason without investing an excess of energy revising page components.

If you need to get your site going as quickly as could be expected under the circumstances, this might be a decent choice for you.

There are various page formats (with various purposes) for the starter designs.

About

Universally handy, with a blend of body text, headers, and pictures.

Contact

These are the Various mixes of structures, maps, addresses, telephone numbers.

Specifics

Generally useful, with a blend of text and pictures masterminded in various segments and lines.

Highlights

Point by point designs for highlights, administrations, or items.

Pictures

These are various designs of picture blocks that make varying display styles. These formats are extraordinary for making the thumbnail route.

Group

It is the traditional format for group pages, including various headshots, names, and profiles.

Others

They are alternatives for showing a menu, a stock rundown/numerous store area, or internet booking.

Page Customization

When you make another page, you can go into the page settings by floating over the page in the left-hand menu and tapping on the gear symbol that shows up on the right-hand side.

Here you can name the page, add a portrayal of the page for Web optimization purposes, cripple it from being open during the working process, give the page a one of a kind URL, set it as your landing page, and even set a secret word on the off chance that you might want to secure the resources on the page.

Blocks

Whenever you've set up the page settings, it's an ideal opportunity to alter your page. You can do this by floating your mouse over the page on the right-hand side of the screen and clicking Alter. Squarespace pages are assembled and tweaked utilizing blocks.

Blocks permit you to add resources to pages. You can

add, move, and join blocks on a page to make a custom design. Each block is intended to add various sorts of resources to most territories of your site.

To add another block, drift your mouse over the left half of your screen, and an additional point (dark teardrop) will show up.

Tap on it to raise the block menu. From that point, you can pick the block you might want to embed and keep on working out the pages on your site.

Here's an overview of all the squares you can include on your page.

Essentials

Text

The Content Block is the essential method for adding text to your site. It permits you to add headings, cites, pre-organized content, connections, and records.

Markdown

The Markdown Block permits you to add text utilizing the Markdown language. To use this square, you ought to know about the Markdown language.

Statement

You can utilize the Statement Block to add styled statements and tributes to your site. Every template has a default format for the Statement Block that can be changed in the Style Menu.

Picture

The Picture Block adds a solitary picture to a blog entry or page.

Video

The Video Block includes a remotely facilitated video to your site. It's critical to take note that Squarespace doesn't uphold the transferred video. While installing a video utilizing a URL, just YouTube, Animoto, Wistia, and Vimeo are upheld. You can utilize the Install Block for other facilitating administrations.

Spacer

The Spacer Block includes a customizable measure of room between blocks. It is an essential strategy for adding and resizing blocks and pictures on a page or blog entry.

Line

The Line Blocks include a flat line between blocks on your site. It is an excellent method to separate content or outwardly separate different components.

Button

You can utilize the Button Block to add tabs and

invitations to act to your site. Button Blocks can connect to the content on your webpage, outer substance, or downloadable documents.

Sound

The Sound Block includes a solo sound record in a player to a blog entry or a page. You can transfer a document from your PC or connection to a remotely facilitated record.

Install

The Install Block includes external resources to your site by utilizing connects to tweets, recordings, etc.

Picture Designs

Banner

The Banner Block shows text over a picture.

Card

The Card Squares adjusts text to one side or right of a picture.

Cover

The Cover Block shows a picture on one side with the text, somewhat covering the picture.

Photo Composition

The Photo Composition Block shows a picture on one side and text over the foundation "card," counterbalancing and covering the picture.

Stack

The Stack Block shows a picture with text beneath.

Displays

Slideshow

The Slideshow Block includes a slideshow of pictures and recordings to a page or blog entry. Clicking a thing will show the following photo or video in the display.

Carousel

The Carousel Block includes displaying pictures and recordings to a page or blog entry in an even strip with no space between the things. The block I utilize to show related blog entries toward the finish of every one of my blog entries.

Matrix

The Matrix Blocks displays pictures and recordings to a page or blog entry in an even lattice.

Stack

The Stack Block includes a display of pictures and recordings to a page or blog entry in a solitary section with one pixel of room between things. It is a wonderful choice if you need guests to look here and there at your display. It's likewise an efficient option in contrast to adding numerous picture blocks on top of one another.

Synopsis

Wall

The Wall Block displays your content in a brickwork style framework. The stonework configuration is becoming progressively mainstream on the web; you've probably observed it previously, as on Pinterest.

It works by situating things in the best format dependent on the accessible space while decreasing any holes, giving it the mosaic's appearance.

Carousel

The Carousel Block displays your resources in a slideshow-like arrangement, with a set number of things all at once and directions for navigation. It is a superb choice on the off chance that you need guests to peruse through any highlighted content in a looking over carousel.

Rundown

The Rundown Block displays your resources in one section with texts and thumbnails on a part each. It is an incredible alternative on the off chance that you need to show existing resources in a direct, exact format that may not be accessible in your template's plan.

Network

The Network Block presents your substance in a consistent framework.

More

Form

Utilize the Form Block to include a structure to a page that gathers data from guests. You can utilize this to make a review, survey, information exchange structures, or application.

Newsletter

The Newsletter Block allows guests to apply for bulletins or get updates to your blog.

Guide

The Guide Block installs a Google Map on your website. It is a terrific method to show the area of your business or function. You can utilize the Plan tab to add tone to your guide to make it stylish.

Code

The Code Block permits you to include a customized code to a page or show code on a page. The Code Block is a decent alternative on the off chance that you need to install an external component on your site.

Menu

You can utilize the Menu Block to show your eatery's menu on your site. It is a fantastic option compared to installing pdf menus on a site, which aren't generally as simplistic website designs as on-page resources.

Squarespace filters the content you include on the menu block for specific arranging. On the off chance that it recognizes examples by the way you entered the content, it changes it into various aspects of the menu.

Schedule

The Schedule Block arranges content assortments into a schedule set by day. You can utilize the Schedule Block to show content from functions, blog, exhibition, items, or collection page.

Keenness

The Keenness Block shows a customer scheduler guests can use to book arrangements.

Zola

The Zola Block permits you to include a wedding vault on your site. It is best for those making a wedding site utilizing Squarespace.

OpenTable

The OpenTable Block includes cafe reservation booking capacities. You'll require your OpenTable Eatery ID.

Bandsintown

Bandsintown show event dates via your Bandsintown created profile.

Channels and Records

Search

The Search Block permits guests to look for content on your site. You can arrange the search block to restore your site results or limit results to one content assortment.

Content Connection

The Content Connection Block makes a visual connection to content assortment or page. It is an excellent method to show content in numerous puts on your site.

Label Cloud

The Label Cloud Block shows labels and classifications from a blog, display, collection, or item page in realistic cloud development. You can show the labels in sequential requests, by weight, or by action.

The Label Cloud Block is an attractive approach to show the subjects of your online journals or displays and gives guests a fascinating choice to find the points you cover. It's entirely expected to put this block in a sidebar.

Archive

The Archive Block shows a coordinated rundown of links related to your content.

Trade

Item

The Item Block includes an item to a page or blog entry. It is an incredible method to advance an item or show items in unexpected blends compared to your Item pages.

Amazon

The Amazon Block shows and connects to a product on Amazon. It is helpful if you partake in Amazon's affiliate scheme.

Donate

The Donate Block permits guests to give to your motivation or association. This Block needs an associated Stripe account.

Outlines

Bar Outline

The Bar Outline Block includes a bar graph in an outwardly engaging manner.

Line Graph

The Line Graph Block includes a line outline in an outwardly engaging manner.

Pie Graph

The Pie Graph Block includes a pie diagram in an outwardly engaging manner.

Social

Twitter

It Shows a feed of your latest tweets and a follow back button.

Foursquare Multitude

Add a feed of your Foursquare registration.

Social Connections

Add social media logos that connect to your online social media profiles. It is another option if your template doesn't have default social media logos.

RSS

Add a connection to the RSS channel or a Blog page.

500px

Add pictures from your 500px record.

Instagram

Add an exhibition of your Instagram photographs.

Flickr

Add an exhibition of your Flickr photographs.

SoundCloud

Install a SoundCloud player.

Considerations to Make When Starting your Block

Moving blocks all over the page can be one of the most baffling pieces of adding resources to your page (mainly for first timers).

Consider the thin dark line that shows up during block movements. This slim dark line will exclusively show where the block will land when you discharge it; the length and direction of the line will demonstrate how the block will look when you discharge it.

For instance, a slim dark line that traverses the whole width of the region you're altering implies the block will take up the entire width of the territory you're transforming.

A slightly dark line that has been shortened will just take up the shortened line's width.

Your Block Customizations

After you've added numerous blocks to a page, you can move the blocks to modify the general look of the page.

You can:

- Move blocks to add segments, columns, or gliding blocks.

- Resize blocks utilizing the Spacer block.

- Stack blocks on top of one another to orchestrate how blocks will show up on cell phones.

While it could be enticing to make a plunge directly into your site's plan, establishing a framework for your site with navigation menus, blocks, and pages will help clients effectively discover their way around your site and upgrade your site's ease of use.

Squarespace gives you numerous choices for blocks and page designs. Yet, when you see all the choices accessible to you, setting up pages and blocks will turn out to be a simple task eventually.

Chapter 5

5 Quick Customization Methods for Your Squarespace Site

It's an obvious fact that I'm a major supporter of Squarespace. It's a phenomenal alternative for entrepreneurs and bloggers who need a primary, delightful stage for building a site. It's versatile, well disposed, and easy to understand.

There is certainly not an enormous expectation to absorb information for sorting out the back-end. Also, on the off chance that you'd prefer to hear me go on the entirety of its advantages, you can read on as I'll explain much more in this chapter.

But since Squarespace templates are excellent, essential, and simple to arrange, numerous clients struggle with designing their site to make it look exceptional.

That is the place where this chapter comes in. I've aggregated the absolute most supportive components I've found for changing up the appearance of a Squarespace site.

A portion of these may be different to you, and some may as of now be incorporated with your templates; however, I trust you're ready to leave with a couple of groundbreaking thoughts for making your Squarespace site your own.

Block Resizing

Numerous individuals who've been utilizing Squarespace for quite a long time won't know about this simple stunt for customization. Yet, it can have a tremendous effect on the format and presence of your site.

Squarespace's simplified features reach out past the block's situation on blog entries and pages; they likewise permit you to resize blocks that are one next to the other.

To change the block's size, essentially drift over the space between two blocks and start hauling toward the path you need it to go in. It works for all blocks, including picture blocks, text blocks, recordings, structures, e.t.c.

For block resizing that involves those blocks that aren't one next to the other, it's regularly useful to use spacers. Spacer blocks make extra negative space and can help include some buffer space between the blocks.

I utilize them regularly to scale back content blocks that range the length of the page and make it simpler for guests to peruse or to give some additional pad between the resources and the angle of the page.

You can likewise resize picture blocks, map blocks,

map block, spacer blocks, and carousel display blocks by utilizing the editing handle for cropping (which is the little dark circle that shows up at the lower part of the block window).

Customizing your Headers

The Style Editor of Squarespace is handy for modifying tones, text styles, and sizes. In case you're a newbie to the stage and need some direction with the Style Editor, Squarespace makes this simple for you.

However, while numerous templates allow you to modify your header's size in the Style Editor, there are a couple of others (Galapagos, for instance) that provide fixed header sizes for you.

Fortunately, an application of a code can work this out if you are good with coding.

Navigation Dropdown Customization

Regarding your template, the color of your dropdown menu may be fixed for you, which can be disappointing when you're attempting to modify your site.

Fortunately, an application of a code can work this out too.

Customize your Buttons, Graphics, and Borders

The ideal approach to tweak your Squarespace site and make it your own is to imbue your image into it, and probably the ideal approaches to do that is through photographs and graphics; they're an extraordinary method to get colors, textual styles, and other visual components of your standard.

I like to add more qualifications to my customer destinations and Squarespace webpage by adding custom catches, infographics, and illustrations. They add more significant character to the pages and make the site more interesting (and I like to think they make it somewhat more enjoyable to cooperate with, as well).

Try not to think little of the measure of customization that can come through photographs and designs. Get innovative with pictures and buttons and use them to produce a befitting site that suits your brand.

Add a Favicon

Customization is all in the subtleties, from your navigation menu color to that smaller picture that shows up alongside your site's name in an internet browser tab.

Dispose of that black box and add a representation of your brand to the internet browser by adding a customized favicon.

In the primary menu, go to Design - Logo, and Title, and under the Web browser Symbol (Favicon) segment, transfer a png document with a background that is translucent (an image with a box around it will not be up to standard).

Remember that favicons don't show up huge on the tab, so go for something concise: a logo, a symbol, or something that doesn't include many details.

By including something even as little as a favicon, your site will be displayed in a professional standard.

There are a few things you can do to change it up on your Squarespace site. All you require is a couple of the tips I've listed, some innovation, and possibly a bit of CSS.

Chapter 6

7 Actions to Take Once your Squarespace Website Goes Live

Your Squarespace website is live at last and ready for everyone to view.

In case you're in any way similar to me, you're most likely to be tremendously feeling good, yet you might have an extra touch of frenzy over what you may have left unfixed prior to launching. So, here are seven actions to take once your Squarespace website goes live.

Essential Information and Business

Your Business Data incorporates your business name, workplace, telephone number, email address, actual area, and business hours. It can be found in **Settings, Business Data, General.**

It is particularly critical to have this rounded out in case you're a physical store. Due to your template, this data may even have its place on your site.

Your Essential Data incorporates your site type and site portrayal. Rounding this up is useful for Search engine optimization, and specific templates will display this on your site. It can be found in **Settings, Essential Information, Site.**

There's likewise a checkbox for permitting Squarespace advancement here as well. If you check this square, you give Squarespace the option to decide to list your site to act as an illustration of the template you've picked.

SEO (Search Engine Optimization)

If you haven't done so effectively, do so by selecting Heading 1, Heading 2, or Heading 3 from the content configuration drop-down menu to coordinate your resources' structure.

Web Search engines usually give headings a top emphasis, so clear headings that depict the resources that make it simpler for web indexes to distinguish the significant subjects of your webpage.

It additionally helps guests all the more effectively filter the page and rapidly discover the data they're searching for.

Likewise, make sure to go into the settings for every individual page on your site and ensure you've finished the **Page Descriptions** and **Titles.**

The **Page Description** and **Title** will be the results produced from search engines. To get the most value for your money here, attempt utilizing keywords that your guests will probably use in their search.

Photos

A decent practice for all sites is to incorporate alt text for each picture transferred.

In addition to the fact that this helps with Web optimization, it also adds to great website composition. The alt text (also known as **Filename** in Squarespace) displays your roll over the picture, attaches it to Pinterest, or for sight strained guests utilizing eyeglasses.

At the point when you transfer a picture to Squarespace, you will discover that Squarespace crops the photo to fit "perfectly" in the format or compartment. Notwithstanding, now and then, the cropping can cut out the piece of the picture that you generally needed to show. That is the reason Squarespace gives central focuses, the little dark circle that shows up over photos you're cropping.

The focal points make it possible for you to control the region of the picture you most need. You should simply go to the photo you'd prefer to alter and drag the little circle to hover over the area you'd choose to feature. It will keep Squarespace from trimming your picture in some unacceptable spot.

A favicon is the little symbols that show up in the window of your browser and your bookmarks. On the off chance that you haven't done so as of now, you'll need to add your logo to serve as your favicon. To do this, explore **Design, Title,** and **Logo**.

You'll need to ensure you picked a symbol/picture that is square in size, with a translucent background not too extensive (since it will be minimal).

You may likewise need to add a social sharing logo, which can be done by exploring **Design, Title,** and **Logo**. The social sharing icon is displayed while connecting/sharing your pages on your various social media accounts.

You should take note of the fact that Facebook and other social communities periodically pull pictures from stored adaptations of your site. Squarespace labels the pictures to enable the social networks to display them, yet social media, not Squarespace, regulates the posted photo's last choice.

Social Media Networks

Numerous Squarespace templates consequently show social media symbols someplace on your site so remember to integrate your accounts to your Squarespace site.

It should be possible by visiting **Settings, Connected Accounts,** and **Site**.

On the off chance that you'd like guests to have the option to stick your pictures onto Pinterest handily, you might need to consider integrating the Pin It button to your site.

It should be possible by visiting **Pinterest Save buttons, Marketing.**

Here you're ready to select if you'd like just your blog or your whole site to display the Pin button and also choose the structure of the buttons.

404 Error Pages

Squarespace permits you to customize your 404 error page when somebody inadvertently explores an old or off base URL on your site. Making a custom 404 page is an excellent method to tell your guests what turned out badly while holding the exceptional style of your site.

Your site is auto-set to utilize the default 404 error page. You can see this default message by exploring **Advanced, Settings**.

To make a custom-made 404 mistake page, make another page in the area **Not Connected**. Add your customized pictures and contents to this page according to your preferences.

For a considerably more creative look, you should seriously consider utilizing a Cover Page to make an innovative 404 mistake page with full-drain pictures, striking features, video background, or buttons coordinating guests back to your landing page.

Since your new page is created, re-visit the **404 Error/Page Not Found** board, tap the drop-down menu and pick the title you want to use to customize your 404 blunder page. At the point when somebody visits a URL that can't be found, they'll currently be diverted to the custom page.

Post Your New Website on Your Social Media Networks

When you're feeling sufficiently sure, remember to refer to your site lunch via your social networks.

There are a lot of imaginative approaches to do this. You may consider facilitating a Facebook or Instagram Live to guide your guests through your new site and how it will impact their lives.

On the off chance that you have week by week or month to month digital broadcasts or online courses, you could likewise go through your cycle of planning or upgrades to your site via your social media networks.

Consider Your Website as Unfinished

Your site is a continuous task. Any website specialist can disclose to you that a site is never fully "completed" or "wrapped up." You can be sure to have overcome a very daunting task by launching your site; however, you will never be finished with the work on your site.

There will be new pages to incorporate, unique contents to add, and photographs and pictures to upload.

Conclusion

As a beginner, I hope you have learnt from reading this book and you can confidently navigate your way around Squarespace. Squarespace is easy to learn and operate with the right information and guidance as we have done in this book.

Reading this book and applying all that is learnt will make you a professional in Squarespace withing few weeks and you will be able to enjoy its numerous benefits. If you are aiming to scale up your business. You should consider making notes of the salient points in this book to your advantage.